# Do Not Devour!
## DEADLY ANIMALS

by Alex Hall

Minneapolis, Minnesota

**Credits**

Cover and title page, © Divingraphy/Shutterstock; 4TL, © Daniel Nahabedian/Adobe Stock; 4B, © Danita Delimont/Shutterstock; 5TL, Pitokung/Adobe Stock; 5MR, © frank60/Shutterstock ; 6, © Kurit afshen/Shutterstock; 7, © kwerry/iStock; 8, © Syed F Abbas/Shutterstock; 9, © A.Jauzi/Shutterstock; 10, © Divingraphy/Shutterstock; 11, © MAKOTO/Adobe Stock; 12, © Dotted Yeti/Shutterstock; 13, © Avalon.red/Alamy; 14, Shutter Etha/Shutterstock; 15, © Natali art collections/Shutterstock; 16, © alonanola/Adobe Stock; 17, © Rob/Adobe Stock; 18, © adriefoto/Shutterstock; 19, © Erica Finstad/i Stock; 20, © Mayumi Kubota/Adobe Stock; 21, © aquapix/Shutterstock; 22, © Steve Byland/AdobeStock; 23, © Ivan Kuzmin/Adobe Stock; 24, © Bjwair/Shutterstock; 25, © mekan/Adobe Stock; 26, © Jez Bennett/Shutterstock; 27, © Kathy Kay/Shutterstock; 28, © aquapix/Shutterstock; 29, © Bevan Goldswain/iStock; 30TL, © Sakis Lazarides/Adobe Stock, 30B, © Enrico/Adobe Stock

**Bearport Publishing Company Product Development Team**

Publisher: Jen Jenson; Director of Product Development: Spencer Brinker; Editorial Director: Allison Juda; Editor: Cole Nelson; Editor: Tiana Tran; Production Editor: Naomi Reich; Art Director: Kim Jones; Designer: Kayla Eggert; Designer: Steve Scheluchin; Production Specialist: Owen Hamlin

Library of Congress Cataloging-in-Publication Data is available at www.loc.gov or upon request from the publisher.

ISBN: 979-8-89577-089-4 (hardcover)
ISBN: 979-8-89577-532-5 (paperback)
ISBN: 979-8-89577-206-5 (ebook)

© 2026 BookLife Publishing
This edition is published by arrangement with BookLife Publishing.

North American adaptations © 2026 Bearport Publishing Company. All rights reserved. No part of this publication may be reproduced in whole or in part, stored in any retrieval system, or transmitted in any form or by any means, electronic, mechanical, photocopying, recording, or otherwise, without written permission from the publisher. Bearport Publishing is a division of FlutterBee Education Group.

For more information, write to Bearport Publishing, 3500 American Blvd W, Suite 150, Bloomington, MN 55431.

# Contents

A World of Killer Critters . . . . . . . 4

Do Not Eat! . . . . . . . . . . . . . 6

Blister Beetle . . . . . . . . . . 8

Nomura's Jellyfish . . . . . . . . 10

Greenland Shark . . . . . . . . . 12

Pufferfish . . . . . . . . . . . 14

Long Arm Octopus . . . . . . . . 16

Blood Clam . . . . . . . . . . 18

Xanthid Crab . . . . . . . . . 20

American Toad . . . . . . . . . 22

Hawksbill Sea Turtle . . . . . . 24

Spur-Winged Goose . . . . . . . 26

The Deadliest to Devour! . . . . . 28

Critters Everywhere . . . . . . . 30

Glossary . . . . . . . . . . . 31

Index . . . . . . . . . . . . . 32

Read More . . . . . . . . . . . 32

Learn More Online . . . . . . . . 32

# A World of Killer Critters

The world is full of wonderful, wild, and dangerous critters! Animals everywhere have lots of different ways to defend themselves, even after death.

Whether an animal looks cozy or killer, it's best to watch out! It might just sting, bite, claw, or squeeze you when you least expect it.

**READ ON TO LEARN MORE ABOUT SOME OF THE WORLD'S SCARIEST ANIMALS TO DEVOUR . . . IF YOU DARE!**

# Do Not Eat!

Some animals make for a tasty meal. *GULP!* But not for long... What makes devouring these animals so dangerous?

After some animals are eaten, their toxins take revenge. These are the poisons inside some plants and animals.

An animal's toxins can be dangerous in many ways. It may cause burning, swelling, and sickness. What makes all this poison even scarier? It can lead to a very painful death!

Let's take a look at some killer critters and score how deadly they are. We'll rate their danger when devoured, their poisonous effects, and if they're toxic to touch. Which animal will win this deadly competition?

# Blister Beetle

The first competitor is the blister beetle. This creepy-crawly can be found all around the world, especially near flowers. Despite its small size, the blister beetle can be deadly.

True to its name, this beetle is known for causing blisters. One touch can lead to burning pain and bumps on the skin.

When eaten, the critter's toxins can lead to vomiting or bloody pee. In extreme cases, a person may develop blistering and bleeding inside their body. *Ouch!* This can be deadly.

## KILLER CRITTER SCORECARD

**BLISTER BEETLE**

| | |
|---|---|
| TOXIC TO TOUCH | 6 |
| DANGER TO EAT | 8 |
| POISON EFFECTS | 4 |

**TOTAL 18**

# Nomura's Jellyfish

The Nomura's jellyfish is one of the largest jellies in the world. In fact, its venom-filled body can grow bigger than a human's! This giant blob terrorizes the waters of China, Korea, and Japan.

In Japan, the Nomura's jellyfish is considered a **delicacy** to eat. Of course, that's only after the jelly is cooked and all its deadly toxins are removed.

Being stung by Nomura jellyfish only causes itching and painful swelling. If a person eats one of these jellies that hasn't been properly cooked, however, the venom can lead to an unpleasant death.

## KILLER CRITTER SCORECARD

**NOMURA'S JELLYFISH**

| TOXIC TO TOUCH | 4 |
| --- | --- |
| DANGER TO EAT | 5 |
| POISON EFFECTS | 8 |

**TOTAL: 17**

# Greenland Shark

Ready to dive? The Greenland shark is found deep in the Arctic Ocean. Some scientists believe this critter can live for as long as 400 years! This makes it one of the longest-living animals on Earth.

When fresh, Greenland shark meat is extremely toxic to eat. Despite its danger, the meat is still a tasty delicacy in Iceland.

The process for preparing Greenland shark is long. It takes several months for the meat to be dried of all its toxic juices. But even when it is prepared properly, the meat can sometimes still make people violently sick.

## KILLER CRITTER SCORECARD

GREENLAND SHARK

| | | |
|---|---|---|
| TOXIC TO TOUCH | 0 | |
| DANGER TO EAT | 9 | |
| POISON EFFECTS | 7 | |

TOTAL 16

# Pufferfish

Watch out for a puffy little fish from tropical oceans around the world. Pufferfish are known for being able to fill their bodies with water and air to puff themselves up.

Pufferfish are full of toxins. So, eating them comes with deadly consequences. Every year, around 50 people in Japan die from pufferfish poisoning.

A single pufferfish has enough toxin to kill 30 adult humans. All it takes is one poisonous drop to make a person's mouth go numb. Too much of the poison can even **paralyze** or kill someone!

## KILLER CRITTER SCORECARD

### PUFFERFISH

| | | |
|---|---|---|
| TOXIC TO TOUCH | 4 | |
| DANGER TO EAT | 6 | |
| POISON EFFECTS | 8 | |

**TOTAL 18**

# Long Arm Octopus

Unlike most killer competitors, this critter does not rely on toxin to kill. But when devoured, the long arm octopus is just as vengeful.

As a dish, the critter is often called live octopus. This is because its arms still wriggle around after it's dead. Dinner is served!

The long arm octopus has rows of suckers on its limbs. When it is eaten, the suckers can stick to the inside of a person's throat and choke them to death.

## KILLER CRITTER SCORECARD

**LONG ARM OCTOPUS**

| | |
|---|---|
| TOXIC TO TOUCH | 0 |
| DANGER TO EAT | 4 |
| POISON EFFECTS | 0 |

**TOTAL: 4**

# Blood Clam

Eating raw clams can make anybody sick, and blood clams are no different. However, that doesn't stop people from dining on these red critters!

The blood clam feeds itself by taking in **nutrients** from the South China Sea, where it lives on the ocean floor. If the water is dirty, this clam will also take in the dangerous **bacteria** in the sea.

Although blood clams are usually safe to eat, they can cause problems if not cooked properly. Blood clams may pass on the dangerous bacteria they've consumed. So, eating the creatures can make people sick or even kill them.

## KILLER CRITTER SCORECARD

**BLOOD CLAM**

| | | |
|---|---|---|
| TOXIC TO TOUCH | 0 | |
| DANGER TO EAT | 3 | |
| POISON EFFECTS | 0 | |

**TOTAL: 3**

# Xanthid Crab

Don't get too close. It's a Xanthid crab! One pinch from its strong pincers will leave a nasty mark. *SNAP, SNAP!* But what really packs a punch is this crab's deadly toxin.

Xanthid crabs are found lurking in **coral reefs**, and their bright colors warn **predators** to stay away. They mostly hide during the day and come out to hunt at night.

A small amount of toxin from the Xanthid crab is strong enough to kill. Unlike some of our other competitors, cooking does not remove these toxins. Stay away!

## KILLER CRITTER SCORECARD

**XANTHID CRAB**

| | | |
|---|---|---|
| TOXIC TO TOUCH | 0 | |
| DANGER TO EAT | 10 | |
| POISON EFFECTS | 10 | |

**TOTAL 20**

# American Toad

The American toad is usually found near shallow water. It hides out during the day to avoid predators. At night, this toad comes out to hunt, snatching up **prey** with its long tongue. *SPLAT!*

Unlike in fairy tales, these toads don't cause warts. Touching their rough skin isn't dangerous on its own. However, anybody who does should be sure to wash their hands after.

Behind their eyes, American toads have **glands** that let out a milky white **substance**. When other animals bite into this critter, this substance can cause trouble. Its toxins can trigger heart problems, trouble breathing, and even **seizures**.

## KILLER CRITTER SCORECARD

AMERICAN TOAD

| | |
|---|---|
| TOXIC TO TOUCH | 0 |
| DANGER TO EAT | 4 |
| POISON EFFECTS | 4 |

TOTAL **8**

# Hawksbill Sea Turtle

The hawksbill sea turtle is named after its beak-like mouth, which looks like a bird's bill. Humans often hunt the critter for its meat. However, sometimes the turtle gets the last laugh.

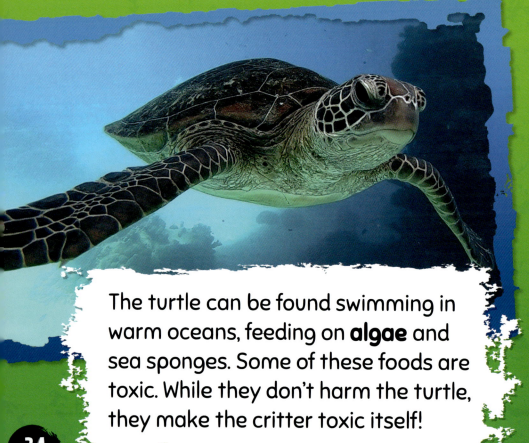

The turtle can be found swimming in warm oceans, feeding on **algae** and sea sponges. Some of these foods are toxic. While they don't harm the turtle, they make the critter toxic itself!

If not cooked properly, hawksbill sea turtle meat can make a person very sick. Some have even died from eating undercooked turtle!

## KILLER CRITTER SCORECARD

**HAWKSBILL SEA TURTLE**

| | |
|---|---|
| TOXIC TO TOUCH | 0 |
| DANGER TO EAT | 2 |
| POISON EFFECTS | 2 |

**TOTAL: 4**

# Spur-Winged Goose

The spur-winged goose is one of the largest species of geese in the world. But its size is not what makes the bird dangerous.

Some spur-winged geese are toxic. This is because of the blister beetles they eat! Without getting sick themselves, these birds pick up the toxin from the beetles.

Cooking does not remove the toxin from spur-winged geese. If someone eats the bird, they may get painful blisters on their body and even die. Luckily, not all spur-winged geese are toxic.

# KILLER CRITTER SCORECARD

**SPUR-WINGED GOOSE**

| | |
|---|---|
| TOXIC TO TOUCH | 0 |
| DANGER TO EAT | 4 |
| POISON EFFECTS | 3 |

**TOTAL 7**

# The Deadliest to Devour!

Who comes out on top in this killer critter competition? The Xanthid crab wins!

While this crab mostly keeps to itself, its strong pincers and unstoppable toxin make it the deadly winner.

A person who eats the Xanthid crab might feel weak and paralyzed. Soon enough, they'd be dead. Yikes!

Unluckily for us, scientists have yet to find a cure for these toxins. The best way to stay safe is to not eat the Xanthid crab.

# Critters Everywhere

The world is a big place, full of amazing animals. But the next time you see a wild critter, do not devour. It might have powerful toxins, strong suckers, or a spiky body!

# Glossary

**algae** plantlike living things that grow in water

**bacteria** tiny living things that are too small to see and can cause diseases

**coral reefs** groups of of rocklike structures formed from the skeletons of sea animals called coral polyps

**delicacy** something that is considered rare or a luxury to eat

**glands** body parts that produce natural chemicals

**nutrients** natural substances that plants and animals need to grow and stay healthy

**paralyze** to lose feeling in a body part or not be able to move it

**predators** animals that hunt and eat other animals

**prey** animals that are hunted and eaten by other animals

**seizures** sudden attacks that can cause a person or animal to shake and even lose consciousness

**substance** a material of a certain kind

# Index

**arms** 16–17
**blisters** 8–9, 26–27
**delicacy** 10, 12
**humans** 10, 15, 24
**meat** 12–13, 24–25
**oceans** 12, 14, 18, 24
**scientists** 12, 29
**skin** 8, 22
**suckers** 17, 30
**toxins** 6–7, 9, 14–16, 20–21, 23, 26, 28–30
**venom** 10–11

# Read More

**Mattern, Joanne.** *Super-Deadly Animals (Super-Incredible Animals).* Mankato, MN: Black Rabbit Books, 2025.

**Musgrave, Ruth A.** *Poisonous and Venomous Animals (DK Super Readers).* New York: DK Publishing, 2023.

**Rose, Rachel.** *The 10 Deadliest Animals (Top 10 Animal Extremes).* Minneapolis: Bearport Publishing Company, 2025.

# Learn More Online

1. Go to **FactSurfer.com** or scan the QR code below.
2. Enter "**Do Not Devour**" into the search box.
3. Click on the cover of this book to see a list of websites.